THE ROYAL
HORTICULTURAL
SOCIETY

A GARDENER'S
FIVE YEAR
RECORD BOOK

F
FRANCES LINCOLN LIMITED
PUBLISHERS

Frances Lincoln Limited
4 Torriano Mews
Torriano Avenue
London NW5 2RZ
www.franceslincoln.com

The Royal Horticultural Society A Gardener's Five Year Record Book
Copyright © Frances Lincoln Limited 2006

Text and illustrations copyright © the Royal Horticultural Society 2006
and printed under licence granted by the Royal Horticultural Society,
Registered Charity number 222879.
Profits from the sale of this book are an important contribution to the
funds raised by the Royal Horticultural Society.
For more information visit our website or call 0845 130 4646.

An interest in gardening is all you need to enjoy being a member
of the RHS.

Website: www.rhs.org.uk

British Library cataloguing-in-publication data
A catalogue record for this book is available from the British Library

ISBN 10: 0-7112-2627-X
ISBN 13: 978-0-7112-2627-2

Printed in China
First Frances Lincoln edition 2006

Front cover
Agapanthus umbellatus, Pierre-Joseph Redouté

Back cover
Love-in-a-mist (Nigella damascena)

Title page
Tulip cultivars

Right
The giant sunflower (Helianthus giganteus)

INTRODUCTION

The illustrations in this book have been taken from the *Phytanthoza Iconographia* (1737–45), the first botanical work published on the continent of Europe to be printed in colour.

The work was compiled by Johann Wilhelm Weinmann (1683–1741), a wealthy apothecary in Regensburg, Germany, who built up a fine collection of botanical art. In the 1730s Weinmann put his collection to use by financing a major publication based on it. The work is in four volumes, alphabetically arranged, and because it was based on a collection of drawings, it is diverse in its styles of illustration. The plates were engraved by Bartholomaeus Seuter and Johann Elias Ridinger, with additions by Johann Jakob Haid. None of the original artists is named but some of the plates may be based on unsigned drawings by Georg Dionysius Ehret (1708–70), one of the greatest botanical artists, whose first important patron was Weinmann. The subtle colours achieved in the mezzotint engravings make the *Phytanthoza* possibly the finest of early colour-printed books.

We hope that you will enjoy making this beautiful book into a growing treasury of notes, observations, plans and reflections, and that it will be a valuable gardening assistant and companion over the next five years and beyond.

Brent Elliott
The Royal Horticultural Society

JANUARY

YEAR		
WEATHER		
PLANTS IN BLOOM		
TASKS		
NOTES		

Hyacinth cultivar (*Hyacinthus orientalis*)

JANUARY

JANUARY

YEAR		
WEATHER		
PLANTS IN BLOOM		
TASKS		
NOTES		

The saffron crocus (*Crocus sativus*)

JANUARY

JANUARY

YEAR		
WEATHER		
PLANTS IN BLOOM		
TASKS		
NOTES		

Hyacinth cultivar (*Hyacinthus orientalis*)

JANUARY

JANUARY

YEAR		
WEATHER		
PLANTS IN BLOOM		
TASKS		
NOTES		

Auricula cultivars (*Primula* x *auricula*)

JANUARY

FEBRUARY

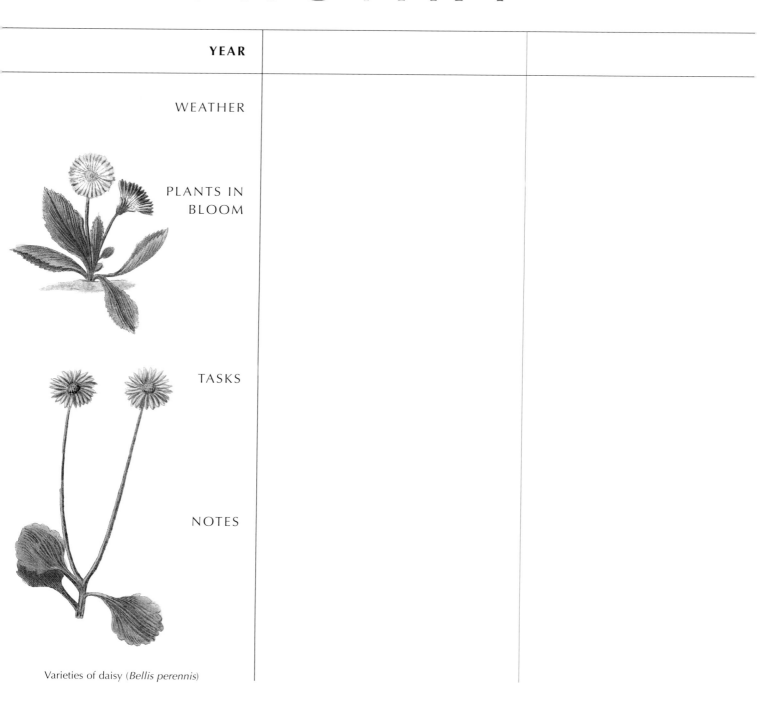

YEAR		
WEATHER		
PLANTS IN BLOOM		
TASKS		
NOTES		

Varieties of daisy (*Bellis perennis*)

FEBRUARY

FEBRUARY

YEAR		
WEATHER		
PLANTS IN BLOOM		
TASKS		
NOTES		

The saffron crocus (*Crocus sativus*)

FEBRUARY

FEBRUARY

YEAR		
WEATHER		
PLANTS IN BLOOM		
TASKS		
NOTES		

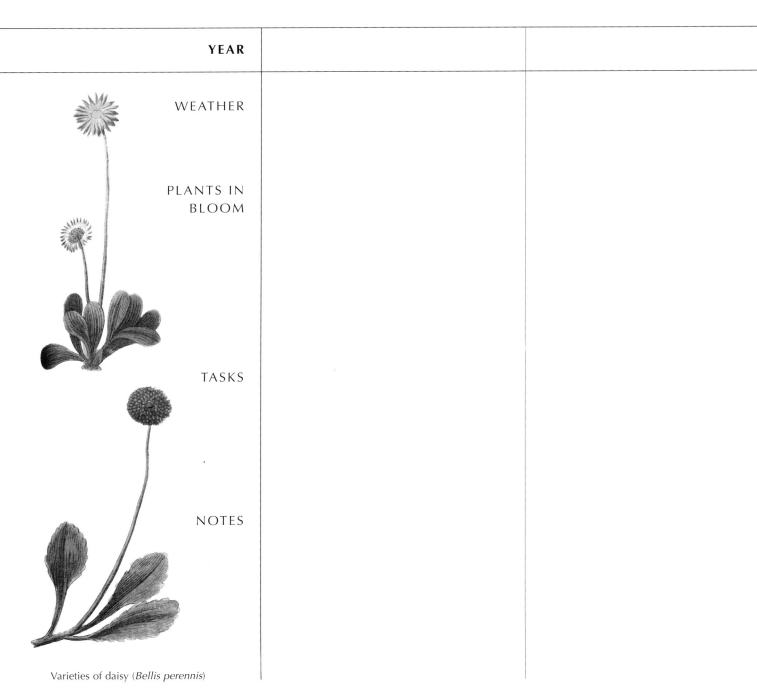

Varieties of daisy (*Bellis perennis*)

FEBRUARY

FEBRUARY

	YEAR		
WEATHER			
PLANTS IN BLOOM			
TASKS			
NOTES			

Cultivars of primrose

FEBRUARY

MARCH

Rush-leaved jonquil (*Narcissus assoanus*)

MARCH

YEAR		
WEATHER		
PLANTS IN BLOOM		
TASKS		
NOTES		

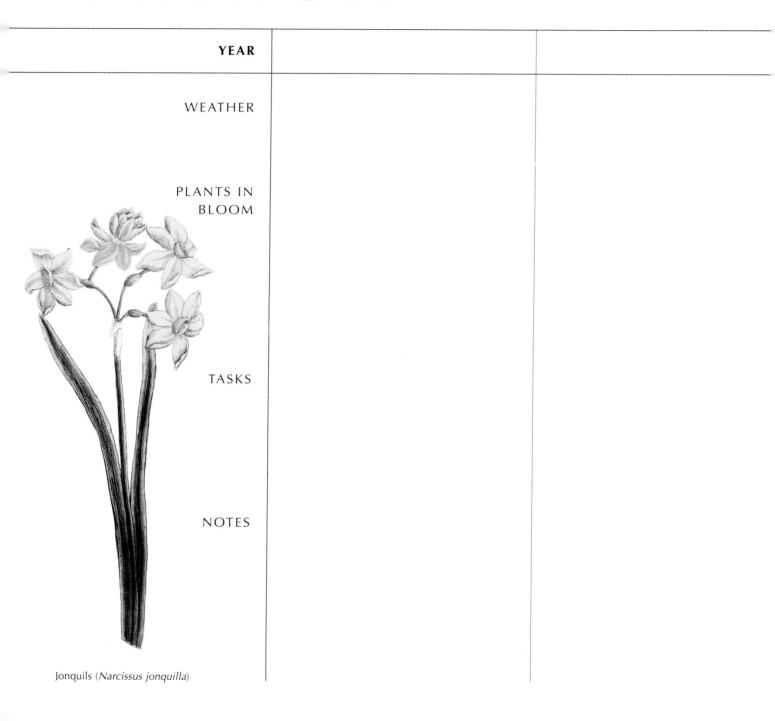

Jonquils (*Narcissus jonquilla*)

MARCH

MARCH

	YEAR		
WEATHER			
PLANTS IN BLOOM			
TASKS			
NOTES			

Anemone cultivars

MARCH

MARCH

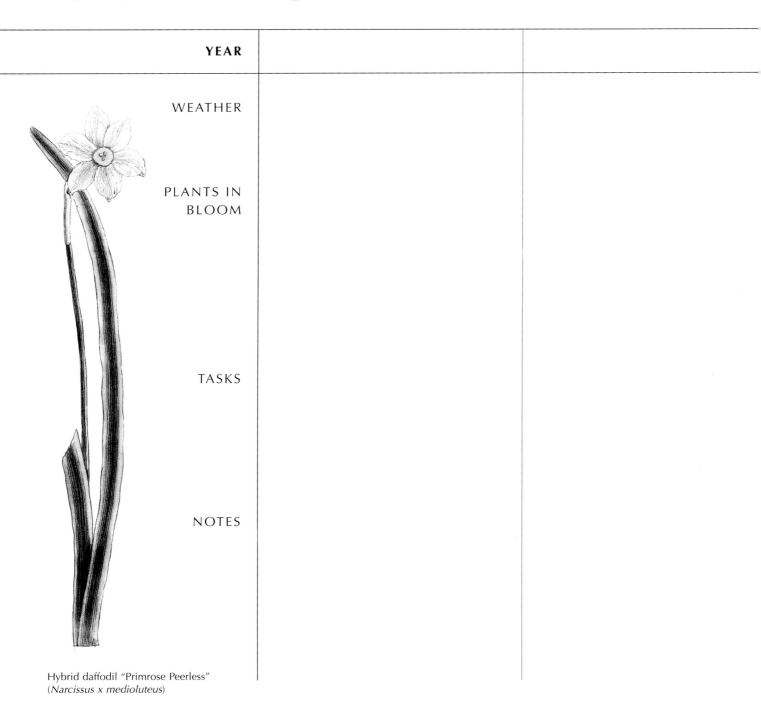

YEAR		
WEATHER		
PLANTS IN BLOOM		
TASKS		
NOTES		

Hybrid daffodil "Primrose Peerless"
(*Narcissus x medioluteus*)

MARCH

APRIL

	YEAR		
WEATHER			
PLANTS IN BLOOM			
TASKS			
NOTES			

Onion cultivar (*Allium cepa*)

APRIL

APRIL

	YEAR		
	WEATHER		
	PLANTS IN BLOOM		
	TASKS		
	NOTES		

Onion cultivar (*Allium cepa*)

APRIL

APRIL

	YEAR	
WEATHER		
PLANTS IN BLOOM		
TASKS		
NOTES		

Tulip cultivar

APRIL

APRIL

	YEAR		
WEATHER			
PLANTS IN BLOOM			
TASKS			
NOTES			

Iris cultivar

APRIL

MAY

YEAR		
WEATHER		
PLANTS IN BLOOM		
TASKS		
NOTES		

Tulip cultivar

MAY

MAY

	YEAR		
WEATHER			
PLANTS IN BLOOM			
TASKS			
NOTES			

Iris cultivars

MAY

MAY

	YEAR		
WEATHER			
PLANTS IN BLOOM			
TASKS			
NOTES			

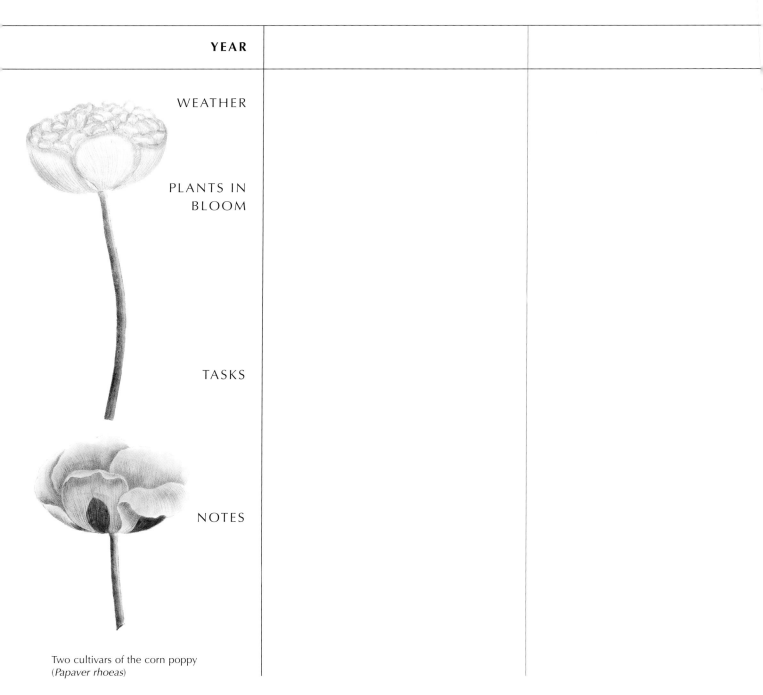

Two cultivars of the corn poppy
(*Papaver rhoeas*)

MAY

MAY

	YEAR		
WEATHER			
PLANTS IN BLOOM			
TASKS			
NOTES			

Two rose cultivars from the eighteenth century, then called 'Milesia' and 'Passe d'Angleterre'

MAY

J U N E

YEAR		
WEATHER		
PLANTS IN BLOOM		
TASKS		
NOTES		

Flowers of tobacco (*Nicotiana*)

JUNE

JUNE

YEAR		
WEATHER		
PLANTS IN BLOOM		
TASKS		
NOTES		

Clove pinks (*Dianthus caryophyllus*)

JUNE

JUNE

YEAR		
WEATHER		
PLANTS IN BLOOM		
TASKS		
NOTES		

The rusty foxglove (*Digitalis ferruginea*)

JUNE

JUNE

	YEAR		
WEATHER			
PLANTS IN BLOOM			
TASKS			
NOTES			

A rose cultivar from the eighteenth century

JUNE

JULY

YEAR		
WEATHER		
PLANTS IN BLOOM		
TASKS		
NOTES		

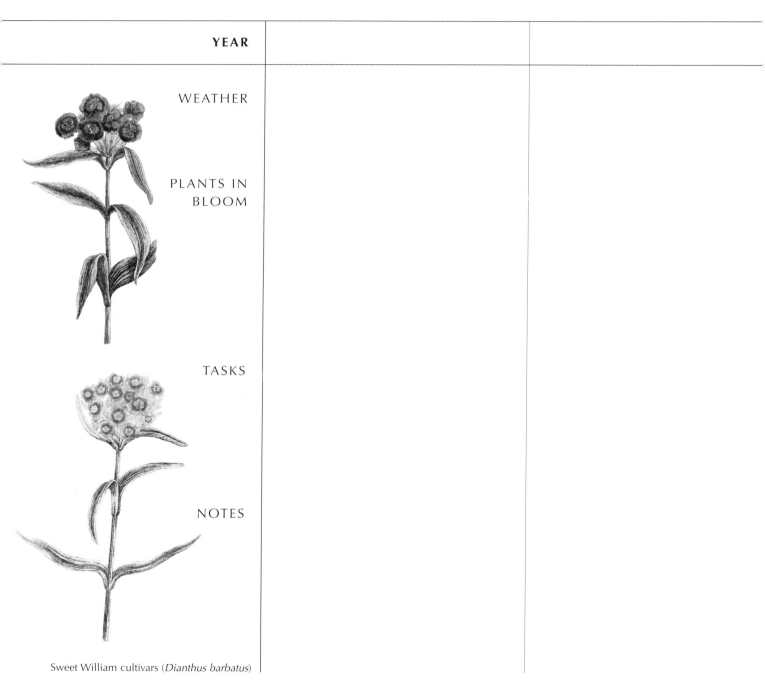

Sweet William cultivars (*Dianthus barbatus*)

JULY

JULY

YEAR		
WEATHER		
PLANTS IN BLOOM		
TASKS		
NOTES		

A white form of the common foxglove
(*Digitalis purpurea*)

JULY

JULY

	YEAR		
	WEATHER		
	PLANTS IN BLOOM		
	TASKS		
	NOTES		

Cornflower cultivars (*Centaurea montana*)

JULY

JULY

YEAR		
WEATHER		
PLANTS IN BLOOM		
TASKS		
NOTES		

Bellflower cultivar (*Campanula* sp.)

JULY

AUGUST

	YEAR		
WEATHER			
PLANTS IN BLOOM			
TASKS			
NOTES			

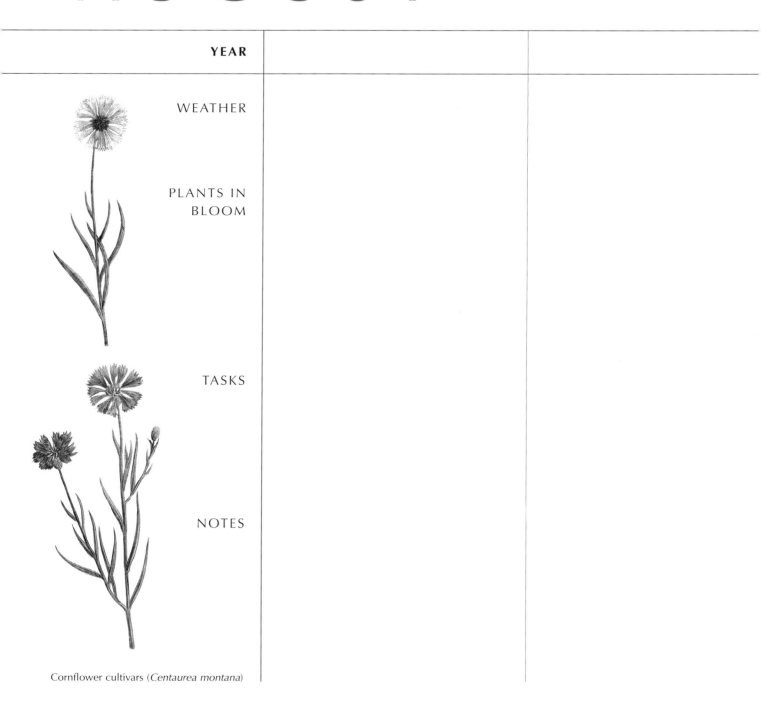

Cornflower cultivars (*Centaurea montana*)

AUGUST

AUGUST

YEAR		
WEATHER		
PLANTS IN BLOOM		
TASKS		
NOTES		

Two forms of *Ajuga pyramidalis*

AUGUST

AUGUST

YEAR		
WEATHER		
PLANTS IN BLOOM		
TASKS		
NOTES		

Ranunculus cultivars

AUGUST

AUGUST

	YEAR		
WEATHER			
PLANTS IN BLOOM			
TASKS			
NOTES			

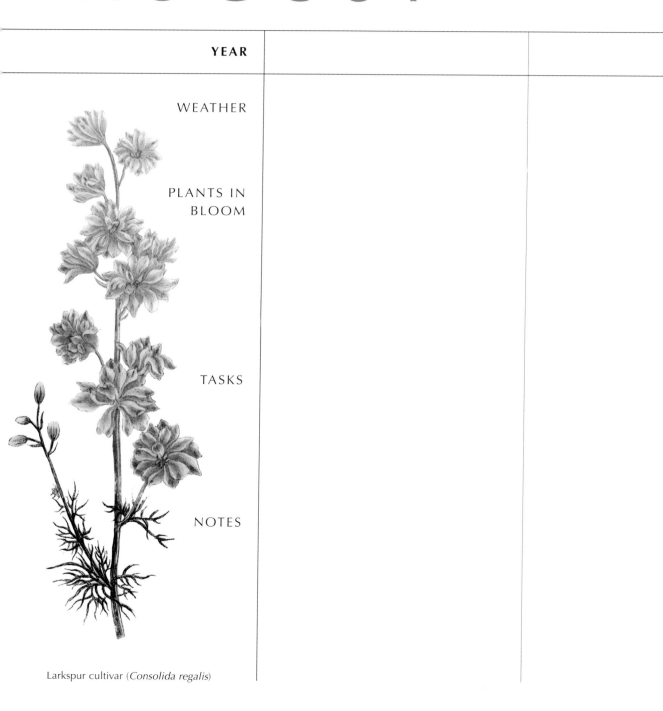

Larkspur cultivar (*Consolida regalis*)

AUGUST

SEPTEMBER

	YEAR		
	WEATHER		
	PLANTS IN BLOOM		
	TASKS		
	NOTES		

Varieties of sage (*Salvia horminum*)

SEPTEMBER

SEPTEMBER

	YEAR	
WEATHER		
PLANTS IN BLOOM		
TASKS		
NOTES		

Cultivars of snapdragon (*Antirrhinum majus*)

SEPTEMBER

SEPTEMBER

	YEAR		
WEATHER			
PLANTS IN BLOOM			
TASKS			
NOTES			

Ranunculus cultivars

SEPTEMBER

SEPTEMBER

	YEAR		
WEATHER			
PLANTS IN BLOOM			
TASKS			
NOTES			

Anemone cultivars

SEPTEMBER

OCTOBER

	YEAR		
	WEATHER		
	PLANTS IN BLOOM		
	TASKS		
	NOTES		

African marigold (*Tagetes*) cultivars

OCTOBER

OCTOBER

	YEAR		
	WEATHER		
	PLANTS IN BLOOM		
	TASKS		
	NOTES		

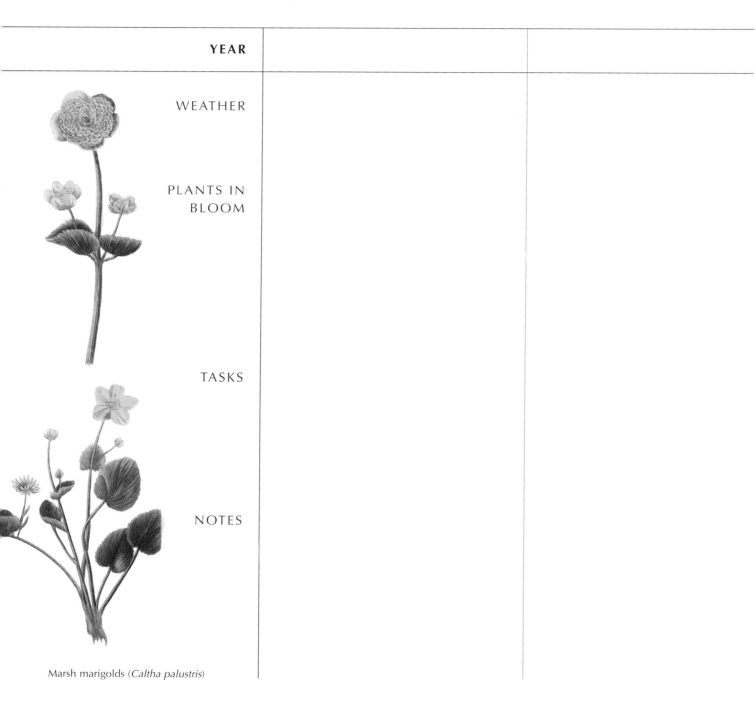

Marsh marigolds (*Caltha palustris*)

OCTOBER

OCTOBER

	YEAR	
WEATHER		
PLANTS IN BLOOM		
TASKS		
NOTES		

Nasturtium cultivars (*Tropaeolum majus*)

OCTOBER

OCTOBER

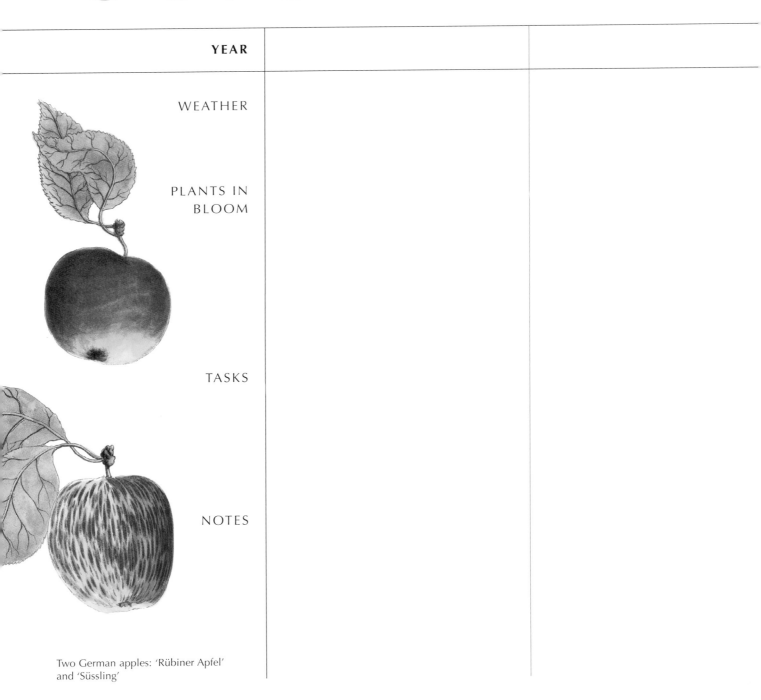

YEAR		
WEATHER		
PLANTS IN BLOOM		
TASKS		
NOTES		

Two German apples: 'Rübiner Apfel' and 'Süssling'

OCTOBER

NOVEMBER

YEAR		
WEATHER		
PLANTS IN BLOOM		
TASKS		
NOTES		

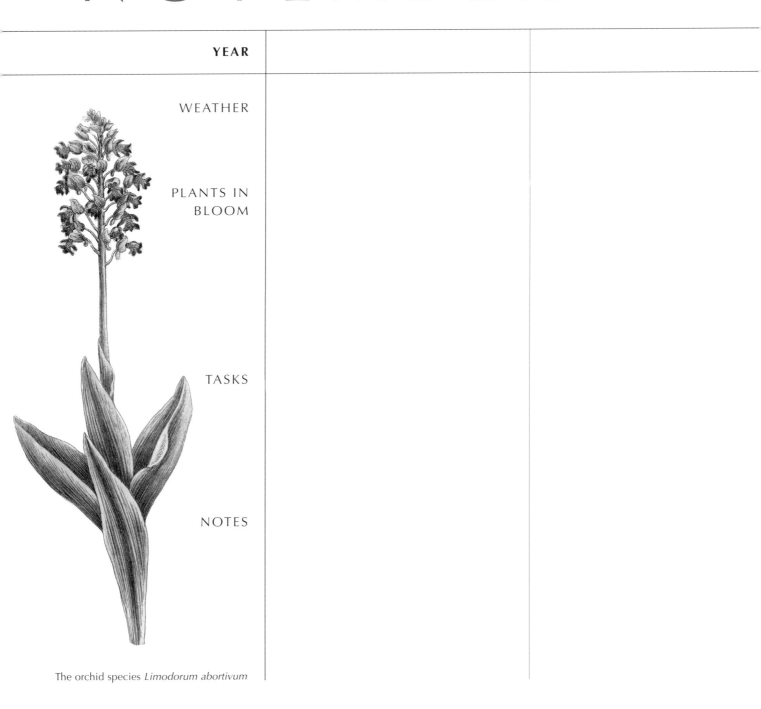

The orchid species *Limodorum abortivum*

NOVEMBER

NOVEMBER

	YEAR	
WEATHER		
PLANTS IN BLOOM		
TASKS		
NOTES		

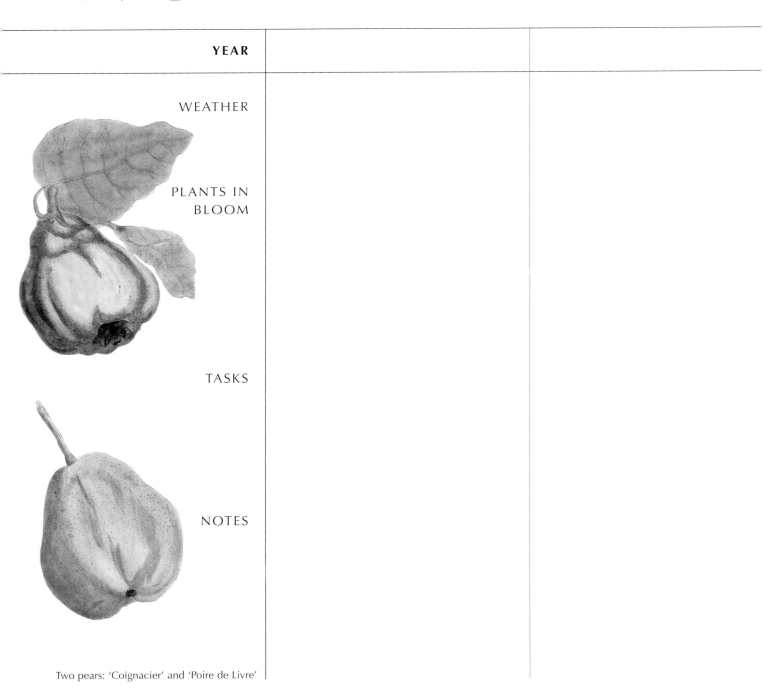

Two pears: 'Coignacier' and 'Poire de Livre'

NOVEMBER

NOVEMBER

YEAR		
WEATHER		
PLANTS IN BLOOM		
TASKS		
NOTES		

Heartsease or Trinity flowers (*Viola tricolor*)

NOVEMBER

NOVEMBER

YEAR		
WEATHER		
PLANTS IN BLOOM		
TASKS		
NOTES		

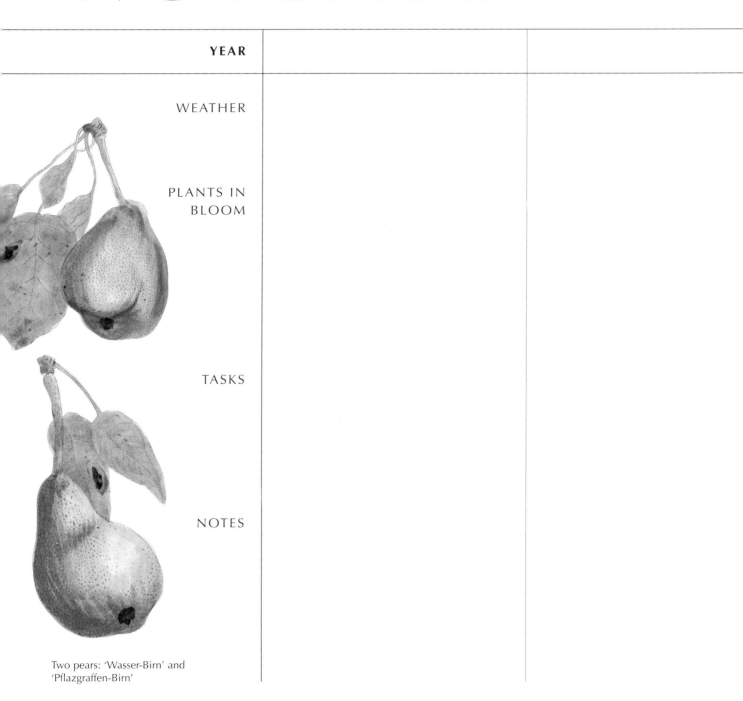

Two pears: 'Wasser-Birn' and
'Pflazgraffen-Birn'

NOVEMBER

DECEMBER

YEAR		
WEATHER		
PLANTS IN BLOOM		
TASKS		
NOTES		

The orchid species *Orchis anthropophora*

DECEMBER

DECEMBER

YEAR		
WEATHER		
PLANTS IN BLOOM		
TASKS		
NOTES		

Heartsease or Trinity flowers (*Viola tricolor*)

DECEMBER

DECEMBER

YEAR		
WEATHER		
PLANTS IN BLOOM		
TASKS		
NOTES		

Hyacinth cultivar (*Hyacinthus orientalis*)

DECEMBER

DECEMBER

YEAR		
WEATHER		
PLANTS IN BLOOM		
TASKS		
NOTES		

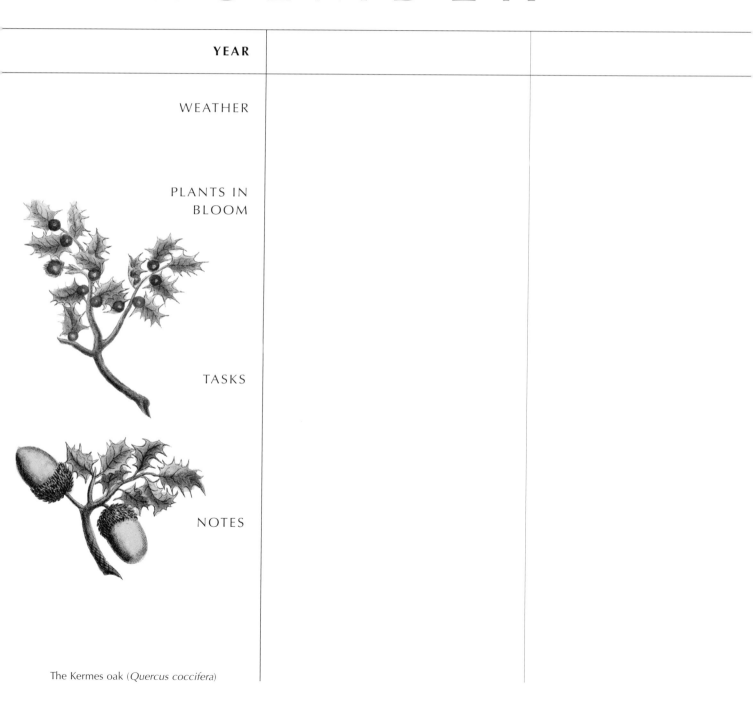

The Kermes oak (*Quercus coccifera*)

DECEMBER

PLANTS TO BUY

PLANT NAME	WHERE SEEN	SUPPLIER	PLANTING POSITION

PLANTS TO BUY

PLANT NAME	WHERE SEEN	SUPPLIER	PLANTING POSITION

PLANTS TO BUY

PLANT NAME	WHERE SEEN	SUPPLIER	PLANTING POSITION

PLANTS TO BUY

PLANT NAME	WHERE SEEN	SUPPLIER	PLANTING POSITION

PLANT SUPPLIERS

NAME	ADDRESS	TEL/FAX/E-MAIL

PLANT SUPPLIERS

NAME	ADDRESS	TEL/FAX/E-MAIL

PLANT SUPPLIERS

NAME	ADDRESS	TEL/FAX/E-MAIL

USEFUL ADDRESSES

NAME	ADDRESS	TEL/FAX/E-MAIL

GARDENS TO VISIT

GARDEN	WHEN TO VISIT	LOOK FOR

GARDENS TO VISIT

DATE VISITED	COMMENTS

GARDENS TO VISIT

GARDEN	WHEN TO VISIT	LOOK FOR

GARDENS TO VISIT

DATE VISITED	COMMENTS

NOTES